Confidence

Simple, Proven Methods to Manage Anxiety and Shyness, and Transform Your Personal and Professional Life

By
James W. Williams

PUBLISHED BY: James W. Williams
Copyright © 2018 All rights reserved.

No part of this publication may be copied, reproduced in any format, by any means, electronic or otherwise, without prior consent from the copyright owner and publisher of this book.

Table of contents

Your Free Gift 4

INTRODUCTION 6

My History with Shyness....................................... 9

Understanding Shyness and Anxiety 11

Coping with Socially Triggered Anxiety and Managing Shyness... 19

Overcoming Shyness in the Workplace 28

Overcoming Anxiety in Social Settings 34

Closing 38

Thank you! 39

Your Free Gift

As a way of saying thanks for your purchase, I wanted to offer you a free bonus E-book called ***Bulletproof Confidence Checklist*** exclusive to the readers of this book.

To get instant access just go to:

https://theartofmastery.com/confidence/

Inside the book, you will discover:
- What is shyness & social anxiety, and the psychology behind it

- Simple yet powerful strategies for overcoming social anxiety
- Breakdown of the traits of what makes a confident person
- Traits you must DESTROY if you want to become confident
- Easy techniques you can implement TODAY to keep the conversation flowing
- Confidence checklist to ensure you're on the right path of self-development

INTRODUCTION

What would it be like to become a confident person and a great conversationalist? How do you get past the paralyzing fear that grips you every time you want to talk to a group of people? Wouldn't it be nice to be at the center of attention for once? If you want to overcome your shyness, take charge of your social life professionally and personally, then read this book. *Confidence: Simple, Proven Methods to Manage Anxiety and Shyness, and Transform Your Personal and Professional Life* explores social anxiety in depth and provides practical tips that will transform your life.

Anxiety and shyness go hand in hand. If you suffer from acute shyness, you are not alone. There are millions of people all over the world who share the same problem. It is a general knowledge that people who suffer from acute shyness tend to live a lonely life, isolated from friends and family. And even those who manage to come out of their shells are only ever really themselves with a handful of people. This doesn't have to be the case with you. What you are holding right now has the power to change your story.

This book is not about a magical formula that can instantly transform you from shy Sean to Brazen Boris overnight. It is based on sound psychological principles that have been applied in regular scenarios by shy people. Each step is detailed and outlined in very uncomplicated terms. While the results vary in degree, the final outcome is an experience of increased confidence in the individual and a more positive outlook on life.

There are many proven ways to overcome shyness and this book addresses the most effective methods. From discovering the real reasons behind your shyness to uncovering mental barriers that keep you from living a fulfilling confident life, this book is designed to peel back the layers of myths and facts about shyness and put you in charge of your life. In this book, you will understand

- The key factors that influences your anxiety and makes you incredibly shy
- 5 reasons why being shy actually makes you a better person
- How to cope with anxiety in stressful situations
- Ways you can make yourself relevant in the workplace
- How to overcome shyness in social settings

This book is not just another self-help manual to swipe off the shelf and store at the bottom of your magazine rack. It explores scientifically proven methods of coping with social anxiety using simple and easy to follow steps that can be applied to day to day scenarios. Essentially, if you are ready to meet the super confident new you, turn over to the next stage to begin your journey.

James W. Williams

My History with Shyness

Shyness is something I have struggled with for a better part of my life. It crippled my effectiveness in the workplace, ruined my relationships with a lot of people I cared about and left me emotionally exhausted even before my day began. I dreaded the thought of going out and interacting with people. I would wake up and within minutes, I was already wishing for the end of the day. Now, I know that this book isn't about me. But, I wanted to start off by saying that if I was able to get past all of this, so can you.

Overcoming shyness for me was a series of steps that I took over the years that gradually built me up to the point where I was very confident in myself and impressed with my social skills. I decided to catalogue that experience and compress it into this book. However, instead of spending all that time in achieving the transformation that I had, I created a point by point agenda that speeds up the process for you. However, I must emphasize here that reading this book is one thing, applying its principles is another. If you want to see a change, you must be willing to do the work.

I wrote this book with the hope that you can see the potential in yourself to be better. Not because there is something wrong with you but because you deserve to be happy. But happiness doesn't just waltz in to your life. You are responsible for creating your own happiness and this book is a roadmap that will guide you to your destination.

Understanding Shyness and Anxiety

Life is full of instabilities and uncertainties. And because of this, we worry about possible outcomes. This is normal and comes with the territory. However, when worries overpower other emotions and interferes with your daily routines, it veers into anxiety. The good thing about anxiety is that it is very easy to diagnose. There are clear symptoms of anxiety and you can make a prognosis without a doctor present. There are mild forms of anxiety and then there are also severe cases. The greater the sense of worry, the greater the anxiety levels.

Shyness on the other hand is a tendency to feel awkward and anxious in social settings especially if it is in an unfamiliar environment with new people. This awkwardness in shy people is rooted in the worry about what other people think about them. Social anxiety stems from low self-esteem and lack of confidence in one's individual abilities, personality, physical traits or even possessions. Shy people almost always have a tendency to project their own insecurities on others. This projection makes it difficult to build new relationships with people. Thankfully, anxiety is easy to treat just as it is easy to diagnose.

SOCIAL DISORDER ANXIETY OR JUST SHYNESS

As I mentioned earlier, there are both mild and extreme cases of anxiety and you might need a little help deciphering what level on the social anxiety scale your anxiety experience falls under. The following are common signs of anxiety;

- Sudden profuse sweating
- Restlessness and a strong urge to flee from the situation
- Rapid heartbeat or palpitations
- A sense of dread and impending doom
- A rush of thoughts [most of which are unwanted]

These are clear signs of anxiety but how can you tell if your shyness is amplified by your anxiety or if you are suffering from a social anxiety disorder? According to statistics, more than 15 million people in America suffer from social anxiety disorder (also known as SAD) which is a form of phobia for social settings. That number quadruples exponentially when you look at the global figures. There are no clear markers for symptoms of SAD other than the fact that all the symptoms mentioned earlier are experienced by the sufferer in varying intense degrees.

Whether you are experiencing the more common form of shyness or you are an SAD sufferer, you are not entirely helpless. By understanding the root of your problems and reversing certain patterns of behavior, you can overcome your shyness and learn to be more confident in social setting. Let us look at how anxiety and shyness affect your life.

NEGATIVE IMPACT OF SHYNESS AND ANXIETY

You may be working with the assumption that your shyness doesn't really hurt anyone but, unless you face what it costs you, it may not be possible to develop the courage to overcome it. I drew up a list of 5 major ways shyness negatively impacts your life

1. It can lead to loneliness

People who are very shy know this well. We tend to keep to our company not because we find ourselves super fascinating (which we do sometimes) but because our shyness keeps us confined to ourselves. Shyness makes it extremely difficult to form satisfying relationships with other people thus causing us to lead lonely lives.

2. Renders you unable to cope in new situations

Nothing sends a shy person running for the hills faster than the prospect of facing a new situation. Even when the current situation is unbearable, a lot of shy people would rather remain in it citing the adage, "better the devil you know than the angel you don't" as their reason.

3. Causes low self-esteem

When in a crowd or small group of people, the predominant thoughts of a shy person is usually negative. Bordering on things like how they are not good enough or dressed well enough and they see these thoughts reflected in the people they interact with even if there is no reason to feel this way. Consistently brooding on negative thoughts like these takes its toll on the individual's self-esteem.

4. Affects your confidence

Having a low opinion of yourself is a one-way ticket down to no-confidence villa. Where you second guess your thoughts, your ideas, your looks and basically everything about you, it becomes even a chore to even summon the courage to get out of bed daily. It is like have a loud cheerleading team inside of your head. Only, instead of cheering you, they are booing you.

5. People get the wrong opinion about you

It is easy for people to meet a person who seems averse to meeting new people and quickly jump into the conclusion that they are snobbish. The fact that you seem to be turning down every invite you get does not help improve that opinion of you either. There are situations that would require you to speak up but, because of your shyness, you don't. Your silence may be misconstrued as consent and your entire perspective on the subject is misunderstood.

But, shyness isn't all doom and gloom. There are positively beautiful traits that shyness breeds in a person and it is important to highlight them here.

1. Shyness make you a great listener

Your tendency to leave the talking to the other party involved can seem like laziness on your part. On the contrary, it creates a sense of trust that makes people want to confide their deepest and most intimate thoughts with you because you listen.

2. It makes you more sensitive to the emotional needs of others

Shy people are experts at observing the people in their environment. And because they are more observant, they pick up on nuances and body language that cues them of the true nature of the emotions these people are experiencing. You may consider yourself invisible in social settings, but invisibility comes with a gift. The ability to see through emotional masks.

3. You are the best kind of friend

It is not easy for you to make friends so when you eventually do, you value your friendships enough to treat them right. You are loyal, caring and sensitive to the needs of your friends and these qualities can be attributed to your shy nature. However, we should not discredit the fact that you are simply an awesome person and once people get to know you, they almost never want to let go.

4. You think before you act (or speak)

Most shy people don't react emotionally. At least not without thinking through their actions before they do. You are rarely caught in a situation where your voice decibel is high and people other than the person you are having a conversation with can hear you. And this is good. People could take lessons from you.

5. You have a calming effect on people

One of the unique personality traits of shy people is that they have learnt the art of internalizing their feelings. So even in stressful situations, they appear calm and collected (they might be a sweltering mess underneath but the keep the chaos there). People see the calmness and tend to mirror that because they are made to feel calmer. Of course, internalizing your feelings is not the best way to go but, for all intents and purposes, it works.s

Coping with Socially Triggered Anxiety and Managing Shyness

We have established what shyness costs you and how it benefits you. To manage the costs and capitalize on the benefits, we need to know how to cope with anxiety that is triggered when you are put in a new social situation thanks to your shyness. But, let us find out why you are shy in the first place. Know the answers to the "whys" could help you better answer the how questions. And it is the answers you get that can put you in the best position to manage your shyness.

Socially triggered anxiety is anxiety that occurs when a shy person is put in new setting where they have to socially interact with other people. We already know the symptoms of anxiety but what are those type of social settings that can cause a person to dread being in them in the first place? Let us start from the simple stuff and build it up from there

1. Eating in public:

You would be amazed at how terrifying the prospect of sitting down in public to eat can be for some people. You ask yourself questions like, am I holding the right utensils? Are there people watching me? Are people judging me as they watch me eat?

2. Public Speaking

If you were to rank the anxiety levels activities like these would cause out of 100%, public speaking would probably be at 110% for most people. Even people who do not have problems with anxiety dread public speaking. For shy people, the feeling of dread is even worse.

3. Leading a group of people

There are people who are recognized as natural born leaders. Those kinds of people are rarely ever shy. They integrate themselves fully into the team, make it a point to recognize the strengths and weaknesses of each team member and then delegate tasks based on this knowledge. Succeeding at leadership would require interaction with people and that right there is a trigger.

4. Asking a girl out

Beautiful girls are gorgeous to look at but terrifying to talk to. And this is not about the girl in question. It is about you. Your fear of rejection makes you anticipate negative responses. You are mostly worried that she is going to say no, and that no could confirm your worst fears about what other people think of you.

5. Standing up for yourself

Shy people are not the confrontational type. Their go-to motto is "let it slide". Even in situations where their emotional well-being is threatened, the thought of standing up against those frustrating them triggers a myriad of anxiety symptoms that can go from mild to extreme.

These are just a few of these scenarios that could make you super nervous like office parties, family reunions or even just getting on a flight. But, why is it that some people are extremely shy and some people are overtly confident? Is it just the luck of the draw or are there biological influences? There are many things that contribute to making a person shy but, we are going to put them in 4 categories.

1. BEHAVIORAL CONDITIONING

They say it takes 21days to form a habit. It only takes the brain a moment to register an event and set up a series of chain reaction that conditions you to act a certain way every time said event occurs. Say for instance, you were on stage as a child and on your way to the stage, you tripped and fell. You brain registers this incident as embarrassing and every time you want to take the stage, you would re-live this embarrassing moment. Over time, you are conditioned to fear the stage and you develop anxiety attacks as soon as you think of getting on stage.

2. INDIVIDUAL THOUGHT PROCESS

My father told me once that a man is the sum total of his thoughts. If you dwell on positive thoughts, you tend to be more positive in your approach to life. You anticipate positive responses, so you are more confident in your reaction to these situations you think about. Negative reasoning elicits negative reactions and negative behavioral patterns. If you are meeting someone for the first time and you focus too much on all the terrible things they might say about you, chances are, you may not follow through on that meeting.

3. SOCIAL CONDITIONING

This has more to do with your upbringing than it has to do with you. The parenting method used by your parent or guardian shapes your social behavior. Children of aggressive and controlling parents who have a habit of criticizing every single thing the child does tend to be painfully shy in their interactions with people. That is because they have been raised to think that they are not good enough and they assume that everyone they meet is also criticizing them. It can take years of therapy and deliberate efforts to rebuild one's confidence after taking years negative criticism from a parent.

4. BIOLOGICAL REASONS

Believe it or not, some people are genetically programmed to be shy. And certain forms of anxiety can be hereditary. It may not be directly inherited from your parents. All you need is just one person in the family to have it and the markers extend to the next generation. It is not fair, but it also does not mean that your life is bound to be one terrible experience after the other. Sure, you may have some challenges and bumps along the way. But if you work at it you could go on to have a very fulfilling life.

Regardless of the reasons you are shy, the good news is that you can reverse the negative effects of shyness. It may not happen overnight, and you may have to push yourself more than a little out of your comfort zone. But, in the end, every little victory you score would make it worth it. However, there are certain self-sabotaging things you might find yourself doing that will impede your ability to make progress. I am going to list out three of them. If you find yourself doing any of these, stop.

Being too self-conscious

When you are constantly self-conscious, you feed on the illusion that people are watching you closely and criticizing you. This makes it difficult to interact with people much less be yourself around them. The reality of the situation is that while it is impossible for everyone to like you, it is just as impossible for everyone to dislike you. Even Satan who happens to be the most evil being in existence has some fans (terrible comparison but I had to go with the worst case scenario here). My point is, spending your time fretting over what people think about you is a wasted effort. Not only do their opinions not count (that is assuming they are talking about you), this kind of thinking is counter productive in building your confidence. Instead, focus on the one person's opinion who matters...yours.

Avoiding new situations

If you have been playing things safe, now is the perfect time to throw caution to the win and take a chance on you. I am not saying that you run off to the nearest cliff and begin a career as a cliff diver (although that would be immensely cool). But, you can't keep putting off things simply because you are afraid. The idea is to gain confidence by overcoming your fears. And, you cannot overcome your fears if you are doing the same things every day. It doesn't have to be something grand. Switching up your sandwich fillings every now and then counts. But, if the activity doesn't really challenge you, you are not doing yourself and favors.

Having negative thoughts

We already talked about negative thoughts and how it causes anxiety. If you want to see more positive results in your life, you are going to have to start thinking positive. Sometimes, people confuse being positive with living in denial. But, there is a huge distinction. Living in denial means seeing the truth but refusing to acknowledge it anyway. Being positive on the other hand is seeing the truth for what it is but making a choice to focus more on the positive attributes. Being a positive person is about making a conscious decision to be happy.

Overcoming Shyness in the Workplace

Your workspace is where you spend a better part of your week. Your interaction with your colleagues could help make your work experience a good one or a terrible one. We have heard horrifying stories of crazy colleagues and nightmare bosses. Some organizations have a toxic work culture that makes it difficult to navigate the workspace, even for the most confident person. That said, you can make a decision to improve your day to day experience at work while building sustainable relationships with your colleagues.

This doesn't mean you have to become BFFs with them. The objective here is to develop cordial relationships that you can capitalize on. This way, you can make more meaningful contributions to the growth of the organization and in so doing, guarantee some personal growths as well. Here are 5 things you can do to get started

1. Make eye contact

Casting your eyes downwards to avoid eye contact might be considered a sign of respect in the animal kingdom but when dealing with humans in a work environment, it is considered a sign of weakness and marks you as ripe for the picking. Studies have proven that people who make eye contact are considered confident, competent and powerful. You want your colleagues to see as these? Then you need to let your eyes do the talking even if you aren't saying much verbally. However, you should learn to work you eye contact making skills because if you keep eye contact for too long, it can quickly go from confident to creepy.

2. Say hello

Walking past your colleague without even as much as a glance or a nod is considered rude and does nothing to help your relationships at work. If not for anything else, just do it to be polite. You would be amazed at how a simple smile and a hello can change relationship dynamics at work. You don't need to launch into a long drawn out conversations. It is about connecting with people. Smiling, waving and saying hello makes you appear friendlier and more outgoing even if you really aren't. And this gives your colleagues a more positive opinion of you.

3. Introduce yourself

There was a time in my life when I would rather jump out of an airplane than walk up to a complete stranger (that I have been working with for months) and introduce myself. It wasn't until an office incident where a delivery package came for me and no one knew who I was. Not even my cubicle mates. I had become so successful at being invisible that I had worked in the firm for over a year and no one knew my full name. In retrospect, it is funny but at the time, it felt sad. If you run into a colleague by the coffee machine, introduce yourself. It is daunting at first, but with practice, it gets better.

4. Ask questions

There is a general misconception that people who ask questions are clueless. Granted, some questions might sound dumb right of the bat, but it is better to ask questions and know for sure than make epic mistakes based on assumptions. Asking the right questions in the workplace can help make you a more effective team player. Plus, it also gives you an opportunity to get to know your colleagues better (professionally speaking). The answers you get can give you insight into their position on a project, equip you with inside knowledge that could benefit you professionally and also enable you proffer the best solutions to problems.

5. Accept challenges

Don't be quick to say no. Your heart may be beating out of your chest and you may be sweating buckets, but challenges present an opportunity to show off your skills and ideas. The truth is, you wouldn't have been approached for the challenge in the first place if there wasn't the belief that you were up to it. Skip the negative thoughts and self-consciousness and focus instead on the task at hand. If the challenge involves working with other colleagues, meet up with your team mates, ask questions and most importantly, show up.

As you take your time working up the courage to start up these tasks I just listed, you should bear in mind that there are situations that require you to not let your shyness silence your voice. Because if you do, you are setting yourself up for failure and disappointment at work.

1. When someone steals your idea for a project

    It is hard to imagine that someone would do this. Unfortunately, it happens more often than you know. You worked hard on a project only for someone else to take full credit for it. This is not okay.

2. When you are being wrongfully accused

    Your reputation is an asset and you need to protect it. If you are being accused of doing something you did not do at work, you need to speak up and correct that information no matter how nervous it makes you. Because, accusations like these can leave a stain

3. When you are being harassed

Sadly, bullies did not stop their antics in high school. They take their sickening behavior to the workplace. And even if the bully is your boss, it does not give them the right to mistreat you. Speak up to the relevant authorities and put the bully in their place.

4. When you have an idea

If you have an idea that could benefit the company, share it. You can do it during meetings, via emails or even a written note. However, you do it, show the company that you are a valuable addition to the team. Plus, it is a major confident boost when your ideas are accepted.

Overcoming Anxiety in Social Settings

When you are in an informal setting, things are a lot more personal. And your dealings in these situations should reflect this. You could be meeting up with friends and families or even chatting up a complete stranger. The goal remains the same. To buildup on existing relationships or to create new ones. It is not always easy but, I will always say this. It is worth it.

1. Stay in the present

When we are in new social environments, our minds have a tendency to drift off to the last painful (not to mention embarrassing) incident. We relive that painful memory and then we start panicking based on this previous experience. This happens even when there are no indications that the past could repeat itself in the present. You need to stop, calm yourself down and keep yourself rooted in the "now". Resist the urge to run and teach yourself to relax.

2. Remove any illusions you have about perfections

There are no perfect situations. You can glimpse perfect moments in between but, there are no perfectly ideal situations. When you have expectations about perfections, you are setting yourself up for disappointment. Instead, keep an open mind. Sure, you want that Thanksgiving dinner to look like something out of movie but in reality, you are getting more of a Bridget Jones vibe at the table. With nosy uncles, squabbling siblings and children tantrums. Go with the flow and keep your humor hat on. This kind of thinking would make things less awkward.

3. Lay off the booze

I can understand the sense in borrowing some liquid courage to keep up your end of the conversation but, if you tip that bottle a little farther than you intended, you could end up becoming the conversation stopper. Alcohol helps you loosen your inhibitions but, that is not the only thing that can be let loose. If you are feeling nervous, admit to it. This allows you to be vulnerable and when you talk from a vulnerable place, there is a high chance that the conversations you have will be genuine. And genuine conversations are key to building meaningful relationships.

4. Try new things

The more accustomed you get to being in new situations, the quicker you adapt when these new situations arise. And with each new social skill you gain, your confidence grows. Do things that interests you. That way, you are even better motivated to take on the challenge. There are also mental benefits to trying out new things. For starters, you open up neurological pathways in your brain. This keeps you mentally fit and reduces your chances of becoming depressed. This positive frame of mind is healthy for your social behavior as people prefer to be around people who are positive minded. The bonus is, you would have tons of stories to share.

Closing

This book may have come to an end, but your journey is just beginning. There are some choices ahead for you to make.

Life is beautiful. Life is also hard. But the interesting thing is you can choose what you would rather dwell on. The beautiful side of life or the hard side of life? Being shy can be limiting in many ways but it can also be a blessing. Today, you have been given the choice to either allow your shyness to interfere with your life's experiences or enrich your life despite your shyness. I want you to be happy and live a fulfilling life. But, no matter how much I want this, you can only have that life if you want it too.

So, here is my final piece of advice to you today. Want more. Don't settle for the shadows when you can play in the light. Don't settle for the crumbs on the floor when you can enjoy the feast at your table. You are made for more and you deserve it.

Thank you!

Before you go, I just wanted to say thank you for purchasing my book.

You could have picked from dozens of other books on the same topic but you took a chance and chose this one.

So, a HUGE thanks to you for getting this book and for reading all the way to the end.

Now I wanted to ask you for a small favor. **Could you please consider posting a review on the platform? Reviews are one of the easiest ways to support the work of independent authors.**

This feedback will help me continue to write the type of books that will help you get the results you want. So if you enjoyed it, please let me know! (-:

Lastly, don't forget to grab a copy of your Free Bonus book *"Bulletproof Confidence Checklist"*. If you want to learn how to overcome shyness and social anxiety and become more confident then this book is for you.

Just go to:
https://theartofmastery.com/confidence/

www.ingramcontent.com/pod-product-compliance
Lightning Source LLC
Chambersburg PA
CBHW060034040426
42333CB00042B/2446